GREAT WHITE SHARKS

by Julie K. Lundgren

A Crabtree Seedlings Book

TABLE OF CONTENTS

CRABTREE
Publishing Company
www.crabtreebooks.com

School-to-Home Support for Caregivers and Teachers

This book helps children grow by letting them practice reading. Here are a few guiding questions to help the reader with building his or her comprehension skills. Possible answers appear here in red.

Before Reading:

• What do I think this book is about?
  • *I think this book is about great white sharks.*
  • *I think this book will tell me what they eat.*

• What do I want to learn about this topic?
  • *I want to learn where great white sharks live.*
  • *I want to learn how many teeth they have.*

During Reading:

• I wonder why...
  • *I wonder what tools are used to study great white sharks.*
  • *I wonder why people kill sharks for their teeth.*

• What have I learned so far?
  • *I have learned that each shark's fin is unique like fingerprints.*
  • *I have learned that they swim in both deep and shallow waters.*

After Reading:

• What details did I learn about this topic?
  • *I have learned that great white sharks are the deadliest hunters in the sea.*
  • *I have learned that they catch and eat rays, sea turtles, and California sea lions.*

• Read the book again and look for the vocabulary words.
  • *I see the word **lurk** on page 6 and the word **dorsal** on page 16.
    The other glossary words are on pages 22 and 23.*

GREAT WHITE SHARKS

Which fish is the deadliest hunter in the sea?

Great white sharks!
They catch big **prey**.

ray

sea
turtle

California
sea lion

FROM THE FILES

Rays, sea turtles, and California sea lions are prey for great whites.

Great whites **lurk** below, then speed to their prey above.

They can feel movement from **distant** animals.

FROM THE FILES

Great whites can see
and hear well.

Sharp **teeth** slice food. Gulp!

They swim in both deep and **shallow** waters.

Tools help us study sharks.

Each shark has a **dorsal** fin that is not like any other shark's.

FROM THE FILES

We know each shark by its fin,
like a fingerprint!

17

People kill sharks for their jaws, teeth, and fins.

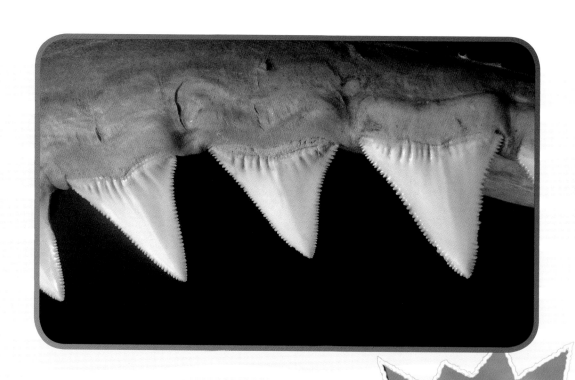

There is much more to learn about great white sharks.

GLOSSARY

distant (DISS-tehnt): Distant animals or objects are far away.

dorsal (DOR-suhl): A dorsal fin is the fin on top of a shark's back.

lurk (LERK): To lurk is to hide in sneaky silence.

prey (PRAY): Prey is any animal hunted and eaten by another animal.

shallow (SHAL-oh): Shallow water is not deep and is often near land.

teeth (TEETH): Teeth are white, bony parts inside a mouth that are used for biting and chewing.

Index

About the Author

Julie K. Lundgren

Julie K. Lundgren grew up near Lake Superior where she reveled in mucking about in the woods, picking berries, and expanding her rock collection. Her interests led her to a degree in biology. She lives in Minnesota with her family.

Websites

www.montereybayaquarium.org/animals/animals-a-to-z/white-shark

www.natgeokids.com/uk/discover/animals/sea-life/great-white-sharks

Crabtree Publishing Company

Written by: Julie K. Lundgren
Designed by: Jennifer Dydyk
Edited by: Kelli Hicks
Proofreader: Melissa Boyce

Photographs:
Shark illustration on cover logo © BATKA/Shutterstock; white shark illustration for "FROM THE FILES" © Dashikka/Shutterstock; Cover photo © Sergey Uryadnikov/Shutterstock; Page 3 © RamonCarretero/istock; page 4 (ray and sea turtle) © richcarey, (sea lion) © GlobalP/istock; page 5 © USO/istock; page 7 © Sergey Uryadnikov/Shutterstock; page 9 © Ramon Carretero/Shutterstock; page 11 © Martin Prochazkacz/Shutterstock; page 12 © Willyam Bradberry/Shutterstock; page 13 © Brent Barnes | Dreamstime.com; page 15 (top) © Stefan Pircher/Shutterstock, (bottom) © OCEARCH/R. Snow; page 17 © Sergey Uryadnikov/Shutterstock; page 18 © Alessandro De Maddalena/Shutterstock; page 19 © Andrey Simonenko | Dreamstime.com; page 21 © USO/istock; page 22 (top photo) © Aerial-motion/Shutterstock

Library and Archives Canada Cataloguing in Publication
Available at the Library and Archives Canada

Library of Congress Cataloging-in-Publication Data
Available at the Library of Congress

Crabtree Publishing Company

www.crabtreebooks.com   1-800-387-7650

Printed in the U.S.A./062021/CG20210401

Copyright © 2022 **CRABTREE PUBLISHING COMPANY**

Published in the United States
Crabtree Publishing
347 Fifth Avenue, Suite 1402-145
New York, NY, 10016

Published in Canada
Crabtree Publishing
616 Welland Ave.
St. Catharines, Ontario L2M 5V6